FOR THE *Love* OF BEING IRISH

IRISH AMERICAN HERITAGE CENTER

Written by **Conor Cunneen**   Illustrated and designed by **Mark Anderson**

The same way that Chicago served as a crossroads attracting the Irish who dug the Illinois and Michigan Canal after digging the Erie Canal in New York and before digging for gold in California the Irish American Heritage Center serves as a vibrant crossroads for the roughly 40 million people of Irish descent in contemporary America, a landmark and a destination in the heart of this country. We care very deeply about the success of *For the Love of Being Irish* because we believe the book offers a fun but insightful portrayal of the core elements of the Irish American experience and identity. It provides an entertaining education on what makes Ireland special and Irish America tick. A departure from pots of gold, green beer, and plastic shamrocks, this project profiles a more meaningful brand for Irish Americans, who have every reason to celebrate the homeland and the indelible impact that this ethnic group has had on the history of America. And for those who are not Irish by birth or descent, the book should encourage an even larger population of those who are Irish by inclination.

—**Tim McDonnell,** Executive Director,
Irish American Heritage Center, Chicago, April 2011

A is for ACTOR

Many a fine Irish actor

Brought to the screen an important factor.

Pierce Brosnan brought cool,

We have charm from O'Toole;

Never a word from any detractor.

The film *MY LEFT FOOT: The Story of Christy Brown* encapsulates all that makes Irish acting, theater, writing, and filmmaking so compelling. Christy Brown was born into a poor, working-class family in 1932 Dublin with severe cerebral palsy.

Encouraged by a loving mother, the incapacitated child learned to communicate through writing and painting with his left foot (and nearly unintelligible speech laced with numerous profanities!).

Christy developed a sufficient skill set to write his autobiography *My Left Foot*, published in 1954.

This funny, poignant work was brought to the screen by Director Jim Sheridan, receiving Oscar nominations for Best Director and Best Screenplay. AND Dublin's Brenda Fricker (Best Supporting Actress) and DANIEL DAY-LEWIS (Best Actor) as Christy Brown took home the gold statuette. Daniel is son of Irish-born Poet Laureate Cecil Day-Lewis.

Ballymena-born Liam Neeson won an Oscar for Schindler's List. He played an Austro-Hungarian-born ethnic German in Poland, from a book written by Australian Thomas Keneally brought to the screen by American Steven Spielberg.

B is for Blarney

When you kiss the stone in County Cork

You'll be talkin' all the way to New York, New York.

You'll talk faster and better,

In a suit or a sweater,

Whether with chopsticks, a knife, or a fork!

The beautiful rustic village of Blarney nestles 5 miles from Cork City, and it is there you can kiss the Blarney Stone. Legend suggests you will then gain the GIFT OF GAB which some say is the Irish ability to spew out voluminous torrents of words without pausing for breath or, alternatively, paint maudlin evocative word-pictures that have the listener crying sorrowful tears into their pint of Guinness, while in the background, someone is singing "Danny Boy" . . . out of tune! Others suggest that the gift of gab and blarney is nothing more than the Irish ability to generate BS. This may be correct in that BS really stands for Brilliant Stories, for which the Irish are famous.

Famous people with Brilliant Stories who kissed the Blarney Stone include Mick Jagger, Laurel & Hardy, and even Bart Simpson—and that's no blarney!

A "banshee" is an Irish ghost or fairy woman. Back in the village, the locals claim you will hear a banshee crying out when someone is about to pass away.

C IS FOR

Craic

(IRISH WORD FOR FUN AND FROLIC—PRONOUNCED "CRACK")

She said we'll have a great **craic**

To the cop who was taken **aback**.

But she meant they'd have fun,

So they romped in the sun

Had a pint and a drink and a **snack**.

Legend has it that many a young Irish visitor to the U.S. has landed themselves in trouble with law-enforcement via phrases like "Jeez, we had great craic (pronounced 'crack') last night," "I'm only here for the craic," and the greeting everyone gives, "How's the craic?"

While the uninitiated law-enforcement officer conjures up evil dens of crack cocaine producing immediate highs (and nasty lows) at a relatively inexpensive cost, our young Irish visitor is simply conjuring immediate highs at a relatively inexpensive cost featuring music, laughter, conversation, and oh, alright, maybe some alcohol.

CEOL, CAINT, AGUS CRAIC (music, conversation, and fun) is a phrase you will often see and experience in Ireland and with Irish friends in Bermuda, Bali, Berlin, or Bel Air.

Famous Irish party animals include Peter O'Toole, Colin Farrell, and Brendan Behan. *"What keeps me here is the rake of beer, the women, and the craic."*
—"McAlpine's Fusiliers" sung by Ronnie Drew and the Dubliners

Ronnie Drew *and* Luke Kelly

ð is for Dublin

Its capital city is Dublin,

Where nuthin' is ever too troublin'.

Where the beer isn't green

But it's great to be seen,

Cos the people in Dublin are bubblin'.

The capital city of Ireland. Home to U2, THE DUBLINERS, Guinness, Thin Lizzy, The Book of Kells, The Gaelic Athletic Association, Ireland's oldest pub (The Brazen Head), and Dail Eireann, the Irish parliament. Location of Leopold Bloom's famous city walk that is celebrated every June 16 by Joyce scholars. Birthplace of that self-same James Joyce, George Bernard Shaw, Oscar Wilde, and yes, The Duke of Wellington, the guy who did Napoleon in at Waterloo. The remains of St. Valentine are enshrined in Whitefriar Church, Dublin.

Dublin is an anglicized version of two Irish words "Dubh Linn" which means "BLACK POOL." Traditionally, the Lord Mayor of Dublin receives the first car registered in Dublin at the beginning of each year.

There are nine cities named Dublin in the US: in New Hampshire, Maryland, Pennsylvania, West Virginia, Indiana, Ohio, Georgia, Texas, and California. Joe O'Connor (brother of magical chanteuse Sinéad) wrote a book about his visit to each of them.

E is for Emerald isle

A prettier country has never been seen

From the Giant's Causeway to Cahirciveen.

There's Cashel, Kinsale, Connemara,

Not forgettin the old hill of Tara,

All friendly and Irish and Green.

Nestled on the west coast of Europe, our mystical, magical island has been designated the Emerald Isle because of its lush green foliage. Okay, let's be honest. That really means green grass—lots and lots and lots of green grass, which you see as you fly over a country that could fit three times into Wyoming!

Millions visit every year to experience the charm and friendliness of The Emerald Isle, the breathtaking Cliffs of Moher, the winding wonderful Ring of Kerry, beautiful Bantry Bay and Beara Penninsula, the mysterious awe-inspiring Giant's Causeway, the enchanting fishing villages of Killybegs and Kinsale (where you will find some of the best restaurants in Europe), Georgian Dublin, the "Garden of Ireland"—Wicklow—and the numerous world-class golf courses populated with lots and lots and lots of . . . green grass. And nowhere, NOWHERE, will any self-respecting Irishman offer you green beer!

"It was great to work in Ireland because it's such a beautiful country, but it's not particularly easy to film in because the weather changes all the time."
—Anjelica Huston

F is for Famine

The Irish Potato Famine

or An Gorta Mór

(The Great Hunger)

"The scenes which presented themselves were such as no tongue or pen can convey the slightest idea of. Six famished and ghastly skeletons, to all appearances dead, were huddled in a corner on some filthy straw, their sole covering what seemed a ragged horsecloth, their wretched legs hanging about, naked above the knees. I approached with horror and found by a low moaning they were alive—they were in fever, four children, a woman and what had once been a man. . . . In a few minutes I was surrounded by at least 200 such phantoms, such frightful spectres as no words can describe, [suffering] either from famine or from fever. Their demoniac yells are still ringing in my ears, and their horrible images are fixed upon my brain."

–Nicholas Cummins, the Magistrate of Cork. Letter published in London Times 12/24/1846

More than one million Irish people died as a result of the potato famine of 1845–1849.

"My son, I loved my native land with energy and pride. Till the blight came over all my crops, my sheep and cattle died . . .
That's the cruel reason I left old Skibbereen." —Traditional Irish song

G IS FOR Guinness

To the Irish, it's more than a **beer**

That much is totally **clear**.

The Black—it tastes great

Drunk early or late

But, oh dear! No car, should you **steer**.

To the millions of loyal imbibers, the dark brew developed by ARTHUR GUINNESS is not just a drink. It is pure magic, a work of art, a culture, a . . . well you get it! First brought to market in 1759, this magical elixir has bewitched and besotted many a stout man and woman ever since.

The pouring of Guinness **IS** an art form, taking 119.5 seconds to pour that perfect pint. But oh, is it worth the wait! And as you sit . . . and as you watch . . . and as you wait . . . and as you wonder at those tiny orphan bubbles swirling and settling around the glass, looking for refuge in some Guinness wonderland and those brown clouds finally, finally morph into a beautiful, creamy black pint that can only be compared to . . . Well, it can't be compared to anything. Because it's . . . magic.

Fact: The author gets REALLY upset if his pint of Guinness is not poured slowly with love and attention.

H IS FOR harp AND the hurley

The Harp and the Hurley and old claddagh **ring**,

Will surely make many an Irish heart **sing**.

From our Emerald Isle

They'll sure make you smile,

They're riches most fit for a **king**.

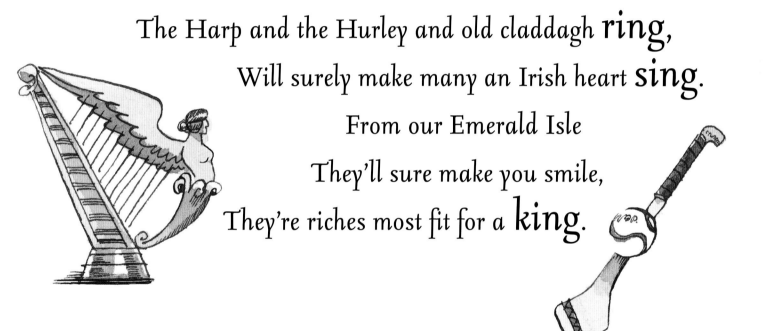

THE HARP THAT APPEARS ON ALL GOVERNMENT STATIONARY and documents is the official seal of the President of Ireland. But just to prove how important this stringed instrument is to Irish culture, the harp is part of the Guinness logo, although it faces in the opposite direction. I guess it makes you think of the Irish politician in the pub who didn't know if he was coming or going!

Every September in Croke Park, Dublin, 80,000 manic, excited fans watch 30 hurley-carrying players from two opposing counties vie for the title of All Ireland Hurling Champions and the honor of bringing the LIAM McCARTHY CUP home for a year. Made from the ash tree, the hurley is an essential part of what has been deemed the fastest outdoor sport in the world.

Hume, John won Nobel Peace Prize in 1998. Heaney, Seamus won Nobel Prize for Literature in 1995. Hansard, Glen won Oscar for Best Original Song 2007.

I is for Irish independence

About the turn of the 17th century, Ireland finally succumbed to English rule. Well, not really! Irish uprisings against a hated conqueror that at various times penalized the Catholic faith, banned education, and tried to destroy Irish culture include:

The Rebellion of 1641
The United Irishmen Rebellion of 1798
The Robert Emmet Rebellion of 1803
The Young Ireland Rebellion 1848
The Fenian Rising 1867
The Easter Rising 1916

All were valiant, inadequate efforts crushed by a powerful English master. Twenty-six counties of Ireland finally gained self-government in 1921 following a savage War of Independence (1919–1921). Ireland remained a Dominion of the British Commonwealth until 1949. The six counties of Northern Ireland remain part of the United Kingdom. Relations between Ireland and England are very cordial today except when we want to stuff them in international rugby or soccer games!

"Early this morning, I signed my death warrant." —Irish freedom fighter Michael Collins (Big Mick) on signing the Treaty with England. His tragic prophecy came through August 22, 1922, in his native County Cork.

michael Collins- (Big mick)

J is for James Joyce

Ireland's finest **voice**

Is Dublin's most famous James **Joyce**.

Humor, pain, and profanity

In his work, you can guarantee;

James Joyce, the critics' Rolls **Royce**.

Two of Joyce's books regularly feature in best novels of the 20th century lists. ***Portrait of the Artist as a Young Man*** and everyone's "favorite"—***Ulysses.*** Here's the truth: If you have read *Ulysses* you are either studying or teaching English literature or you are extraordinarily patient as you grapple with his stream of consciousness form of writing. The trick is to listen to a reading of the book by professional actors—preferably Irish. Then, you can appreciate the pacing, fun, warmth, the wonderful witty dialogue, and (ahem) pretty filthy mind of the Jesuit-educated writer.

One of the joys of visiting Dublin is to take a guided tour through many of the locations cited by Joyce, who was born in Ireland's capital in 1882, lived much of his life in Italy, and died in Zurich, where he is buried, in 1941.

Jameson is Ireland's best selling whiskey. The Local, an Irish pub in Minneapolis, serves more Jameson than any other pub in the world, yet only 7 percent of the city claim Irish ancestry. Obviously 93 percent wish!

k is for

book of Kells

Brother Patrick, Brother Patrick—Good Heaven!

There's a typo on page one eleven.

Though your arm's in a splint

Yes, we need a reprint

Says our Brother Superior, Big Kevin.

Dublin's historic Trinity College is home to the Book of Kells, Ireland's foremost national treasure. To say it was written in the 9th century belies the creativity, ornate work, and gorgeous illustrations that make up this magnificent Latin rendition of the four gospels. Pages measuring 13 by 9½ inches were crafted on vellum by the Columban monks. The book was written—nay, crafted—either on the small island of Iona at St Colum Cille's monastery or at a Kells, County Meath, monastery, where it was housed for many years.

More than 500,000 visitors see the book each year in the OLD LIBRARY AT TRINITY COLLEGE. It is a must-see for any visitor to Ireland.

Thomas Kavanagh (Dublin), Patrick Kelly (Mayo), Michael Kenny (Galway), Myles Keogh (Carlow), and Dennis Kerr (Antrim) died with George Custer at the Battle of Little Big Horn, June 25, 1876.

L is for Luck of the Irish

The Irish are lucky, they say
Though history might suggest that's a nay.
We had the Brits for a while;
Man! They cramped our style.
But with them we now work and play.

JOHN LENNON wrote that if you had the luck of the Irish "you'd be sorry and wish you were dead." Many who suffered through English invasion, dreadful potato famine, or Black and Tan terror would concur. Some might even suggest that the country song lyrics "If it wasn't for bad luck, I'd have no luck at all" were surely written for an Irish cowboy! Exactly where the phrase originated is unclear, but one person who might believe that the luck of the Irish is a positive is Limerick's DOLORES MCNAMARA who won what was then (2005) Europe's largest lottery of €126 million.

The four-leaf clover, which is NOT a shamrock (a shamrock has only 3 leaves) is reputed to bring good luck. Although sometimes seen as mischievous, in Irish folklore the leprechaun brings good luck and well-being to people.

"And there's no luck about a house
If it lack honesty." —W.B. Yeats, "The Ghost of Roger Casement"

N IS FOR No irish need apply

Jobs for all, jobs for all

But hey Paddy! Don't bother to call.

No Irish need apply;

Yes, you might wonder why.

They're the finest workers of all.

No less a person than **W.E.B. DUBOIS**, famed civil rights activist and founding member of the National Association for the Advancement of Colored People, said that the first time he truly understood discrimination was when he saw how the Irish were treated. In many parts of the southern United States, slaves—who were seen as property by their owners—were treated better than Irish laborers.

The Irish were marginalized because of their Catholic faith, anti-English (read anti-WASP) attitude, and a perception—which we may have helped—that we liked a drink now and again.

As the Irish slowly infiltrated politics, police, unions, corporate America, and finally Wall Street, the rampant racism that impacted the Irish faded. When campaigning for the White House, John F. Kennedy paid no attention to No Irish Need Apply!

Today, Dublin hosts the European headquarters for Google, Facebook, and LinkedIn.

O is for

O'connell (daniel)

Working for Catholic **emancipation**

It was his life's **aspiration**.

His heart buried in Rome,

But Kerry was home;

Not England, an **alien nation**.

For much of the period prior to the Catholic Emancipation Act of 1829, Irish Catholics suffered a Jim Crow–type environment under so called Penal Laws enacted by English rule. At various times, CATHOLICS WERE PREVENTED FROM VOTING or holding office, educating their children abroad (if they could afford it), and the Irish language was banned in schools.

Kerry-born DANIEL O'CONNELL, a long time agitator for Catholic rights, won a County Clare election to the British House of Commons. All Members of Parliament were obliged to swear allegiance to the head of the Church of England (the monarch), which O'Connell refused to do. Ultimately, O'Connell forced repeal of the law, thus allowing Catholic emancipation and why he is known as The Great Emancipator.

The "O" in Irish names like O'Brien, O'Flaherty, and O'Connor is a derivation of the Irish word "Ua" meaning grandson or descendant.

p IS FOR

Politics

Vote early and often he **said**,

Maybe the living and also the **dead**.

For if you want your best selection

To win the next election,

Vote twice from your funeral **bed**!

JOHN FITZGERALD KENNEDY and RONALD REAGAN were the two most "Irish" of presidents. Kennedy, was born into ill-gotten wealth generated by the Catholic, but hardly saintly Joe Kennedy. Reagan was born to an impoverished, alcoholic father and caring mother. Kennedy: the charmer who was not always bound by marriage vows. Reagan: the raconteur, often of ethnic, profane stories that he shared with Irish American politicians including Daniel Patrick Moynihan.

Paradoxically, the "Great Communicator" Reagan, who exuded warmth to the American people, had poor relationships with family members. Kennedy visited Ireland immediately after his "Ich Bin Ein Berliner" speech at the Berlin Wall. Although never embraced as warmly by the Irish, Reagan received a rapturous reception when he visited his ancestral home at Ballyporeen, County Tipperary, in 1984.

"They have vilified me, they have crucified me. Yes, they have even criticized me." —"Hizzoner" Richard J. Daley, "Da Mare," Chicago 1955–1976

"If this nation had achieved its present political and economic stature a century or so ago, my great grandfather might never have left New Ross, and I might, if fortunate, be sitting down there with you. Of course if your own president* had never left Brooklyn, he might be standing up here instead of me."

JFK to Dáil Éireann (Irish Parliament) June 28, 1963

*Eamonn de Valera (1882–1975), president of Ireland 1959–1973 and one of the leaders of the 1916 rising, was born in New York.

Q is for

the Quiet man

A red-headed Maureen O'Hara.

Was filmed in West Connemara.

Directed by Ford,

John Wayne she adored—

A love hotter than the Sahara.

In Ireland, everyone wishes you a "top o' the morning," you'll find a pot of gold at the end of the rainbow, and leprechauns dance on mushrooms while a roguish horse-trader will try and sell you the same horse twice before encouraging you to buy a pint of Guinness and "another one for the brother—he'll be here soon" before telling you that he has to go home to "the little woman."

Or at least that is what *The Quiet Man*, JOHN FORD'S homage to his ancestral home, would have you believe. Although, hardly an accurate depiction of Ireland, the 1952 movie is probably the best tourist commercial ever for the Emerald Isle. Filmed in County Mayo on the grounds of luxurious Ashford Castle, the magnificent scenery combined with cleverly written romantic comedy encouraged generations of Irish Americans to visit the land of their parents.

R is for Riverdance

Moving faster than Dasher and Prancer

Was there ever a better man dancer?

He'd do a jig and a reel

With those ankles of steel—

Mike Flatley, the Irish romancer.

Riverdance originated as a seven-minute interval piece during the 1994 Eurovision song contest in Dublin. This contemporary interpretation of Irish dance does not always sit well with traditionalists, but the combination of modern Irish music, high-kicking dancers, superb choreography, and (God help us all) two sexy dancers in Michael Flatley and JEAN BUTLER generated an international sensation. The seven-minute piece morphed into a full-length theatrical show produced by husband-and-wife team, JOHN McCOLGAN and MOYA DOHERTY with music by Bill Whelan. Michael Flatley, who is a Guinness World Records entrant for 35 taps per second, left the show in a fit of commercial and artistic angst to start his own immensely successful show *Lord of the Dance.*

"As I was goin' over the Cork and Kerry mountains, I met with Captain Farrell and his money he was counting." —"Whiskey in the Jar," Irish traditional song about a roguish robber

S is for
St. Patrick
Shamrock

He's our patron saint,

Which is really quite quaint.

He brought us the faith,

Made us holy and great

But Irish? St. Patrick? He ain't!

St. Patrick's first visit to Ireland did not exactly evoke images of "IRELAND OF THE WELCOMES." Captured by marauding Irish warriors, the Welsh- or Scottish-born 16-year-old spent about six years in Ireland as a slave. After his escape, precipitated by a voice from God telling him to leave, he became a priest. He then returned to Ireland bringing the Catholic faith, and legend has it, drove the snakes out of Ireland!

Another legend suggests that St. Patrick used the shamrock to illustrate the mystery of the Holy Trinity and how three could be one. Today the shamrock is probably the fastest way for the stranger to appreciate an Irish association. You will find the shamrock adorning Aer Lingus planes, Glasgow Celtic jerseys, and the windows of Irish pubs from Maine to Madrid.

Galway-born Sister Sarah Clarke (1919–2002) was dubbed the "Joan of Arc of English jails" for her tireless work to free the Guildford Four, Birmingham Six, and many others.

T IS FOR  *Titanic*

In the early hours of April 15, 1912, while on its maiden voyage, the "unsinkable" *Titanic* hit an iceberg, sending more than 1,500 people to their doom in the freezing waters of the North Atlantic. The ship was built at Belfast's Harland & Wolff shipyards under the direction of County Down–born naval architect Thomas Andrews, who perished with the ship. He was one of an estimated 140 Irish people on the doomed vessel.

Billed as the largest passenger ship in the world, *Titanic*'s final point of departure was Cobh (then Queenstown), County Cork, where a number of emigrating Irish boarded as third-class passengers.

Interest in the *Titanic* has grown in recent years due to the success of the movie *Titanic* (where even Leonardo DiCaprio died!) and the discovery of its final resting place by oceanographer Robert Ballard in 1985.

Bewley's famous Dublin Tea House, described by poet Brendan Kennelly as the "heart and hearth of Dublin," provided comfort to literature greats like Brendan Behan and Patrick Kavanagh.

u is for U2

Yes indeed—it's a Beautiful Day

When you've tickets to see U2 play.

Whether Bangalore, Budapest, Bantry, or Bari

Bono, the Edge, cool Adam, and Larry

Will have you rockin' 'n' rollin' okay!

When aspiring drummer LARRY MULLEN posted a note on his school notice board in 1976 seeking members for a new band, the result was U2—BONO (Paul Hewson), EDGE (Dave Evans), ADAM CLAYTON, and Mullen. Manager PAUL McGUINNESS, who has been with the band almost from the outset, is the "fifth" member.

When the young Bono launched into "I Will Follow" (still a band staple) on their 1980 debut album *Boy*, few would have imagined that the band would rival The Rolling Stones and Bruce Springsteen as the biggest rock act in the world.

While the rest of the band live the life of respectable, middle-aged rock stars, between tours, Bono continues to push, prod, annoy, and irritate anyone who will listen (including Bush, Obama, Mandela, Oprah) as he strives to reduce poverty and AIDS in Africa.

Undertones lead singer Feargal Sharkey in 2010 was awarded Doctor of Letters (DLitt) from the University of Ulster for his services to music.

V IS FOR

Vikings

They came from across the water

Looking for your wealth, your son, or your daughter.

They were known as the Vikings,

And they fought with our High Kings

With often a terrible slaughter.

before England invaded, we had the Normans, and before the Normans, we had the Vikings! These were a group of not-very-friendly characters from various parts of Scandinavia. When Olaf and Bjorn and Benny and their rather aggressive fellow Norsemen disembarked their longships in Ireland around 795, they did not bring the same love their fellow brethren ABBA gushed about years later.

Many Vikings eventually succumbed to the charms of bashful Irish colleens and settled in Ireland. Their influence has been immense. The first permanent settlements at Dublin, Waterford, and Limerick were founded by these boisterous, bearded lads. Many of them met their end when defeated by BRIAN BORU, High King of Ireland, at the Battle of Clontarf (on the outskirts of Dublin) Good Friday 1014. Legend has it that Brian Boru—while praying in his tent after the victory—was killed by the Viking Brodir.

The little village of Virginia in the lake country of County Cavan has twice won Ireland's Tidy Town of the Year.

"I can resist anything but temptation."

—Oscar Wilde

W is for Wilde

The Importance of Being Earnest

May well be his best.

Never modest or quiet

His life was a riot.

He truly loved life with great zest.

"ANYTHING TO DECLARE?" "NOTHING BUT MY GENIUS," said the accurate, but hardly modest Oscar Wilde to the U.S. Customs officer. A man of extraordinary creativity, a smart-aleck: "The difference between men and women—I cannot conceive." He believed Southerners compared everything to pre-Civil-War days: "How beautiful the moon is tonight," to which the Southern belle responded, "Yes, but you should have seen it before the war!" Cynical about marriage: "Men marry because they are tired. Women because they are curious. Both are disappointed." He was a wonderful satirist of the upper class who died destitute, at the age of 46 in Paris.

Yeats wrote that Wilde's material seemed to have been written "overnight with labour and yet all spontaneous."

X is for

Exile

Mamma, it's only for a **while**,

He said with a sad, sad **smile**.

But not another word was spoken

For her dear old heart was broken;

Another son and child for **exile**.

The history of Ireland is one of consistent, ongoing emigration that bled this blessed land dry of many of its youth and much of its energy. Some left because of defeat in battle, as with the famous Wild Geese led by PATRICK SARSFIELD who exiled to France about 1691. But the emigration hemorrhage exploded following the famine year of 1847. The Irish population literally almost halved, to 4.5 million people, between 1847–1900.

While many traveled to Australia and Canada, the vast majority of Irish exiles travelled to the "SHORES OF AMERIKAY." It is estimated that close to 200,000 emigrated from Ireland each year from 1847 to 1850, which is how the Irish became a force in U.S. politics; why the Chicago river is dyed green; and why every politician claims to be Irish on St. Patrick's Day.

X-rated! Movies banned in Ireland include Monty Python's Life of Brian, Ulysses, and Natural Born Killers.

Y is for

Yeats

To poetry, he's a bit like Bill Gates

Is Ireland's William B. Yeats.

The Abbey Theater, he founded

As a man, he was grounded

Truly, William was one of the greats.

WILLIAM BUTLER YEATS is the brightest light in the pantheon of a stellar range of Irish poets and playwrights, not least of whom are Seamus Heaney, Brian Friel, Antoine Ó Raifteiri, John B. Keane, Hugh Leonard, and Oscar Wilde.

Yeats' heritage lives on not just in his lyrical poetry and evocative imagery: as one of the founders of Dublin's famed Abbey Theatre, he ensured that Irish literature and drama would have a welcome and nurturing home.

On receipt of the Nobel Prize for Literature in 1923, for poems such as "The Wild Swans at Coole," "Easter 1916," "To a Child Dancing in the Wind," and "The Lake Isle of Inishfree," he said "that this honor has come to me less as an individual than as a representative of Irish literature."

Sir Walter Raleigh, responsible for bringing tobacco back from The New World was Mayor of Youghal, County Cork in 1558.

Z IS FOR Zigzag

IRISH ROADS

The farmer said with kindly good cheer

If I were you, I wouldn't start from here.

See—with these zigzag roads,

Of which we've got loads,

It's better to start over there.

If we were to tell you where the longest, windiest road in Ireland is, we'd probably have to kill you—but with kindness! Here's a little tip to help you find that narrow stretch of road, bordered by blackberry-filled hedgerow, overlooked by sleepy cattle. It leads to a local church and adjacent pub with grocery store attached reminiscent of the magical Ring of Kerry. It lies somewhere west of the majestic Hill of Howth, north of beautiful Bantry Bay, East of West Connemara, and south of Royal Portrush Golf Club, where Graeme McDowell is an honorary life member.

And if you can't find the longest, windiest road in Ireland, well then, just park the car, order a pint of Guinness or your favorite tipple, savor some of Mrs. Murphy's soda bread and freshly caught salmon while listening to the Chieftains playing "The Rocky Road to Dublin" and thank the Good Lord for THE LOVE OF BEING IRISH.

Zanta, a white rhinoceros native to Zimbabwe, takes her zzzz's at Dublin Zoo.

Text copyright © 2011 by Conor Cunneen

Illustrated and designed by Mark Anderson

This book is available in quantity at special discounts for your group or organization. For further information, contact:

Triumph Books

542 South Dearborn Street

Suite 750

Chicago, Illinois 60605

312. 939. 3330

Fax 312. 663. 3557

www.triumphbooks.com

Printed in China

ISBN 978–1–60078–596–2